# ZEN IN THE ART OF SURGERY

SAAD SHAIKH

Copyright © 2021 by Saad Shaikh
All rights reserved

Published in the United States by
The Well-Tempered Library

ISBN: 978-0692702796 (Print & Ebook)
979-8761808416 (Hardcover)

FOURTH EDITION

Book & Cover Design by the Author

*For the universe . . .*

*The value of teaching without words and accomplishing without action is understood by few in the world.*

LAO TZU

# CONTENTS

| | |
|---|---|
| *Prologue* | 9 |
| AWARENESS | 13 |
| WU WEI | 21 |
| UNCERTAINTY | 30 |
| STORIES | 37 |
| BREATH | 45 |
| POSTURE | 61 |
| KARMA | 67 |
| MISTAKES | 73 |
| INTERDEPENDENCE | 82 |
| ABSOLUTION | 88 |
| INTUITION | 92 |
| BUDDHA | 101 |
| *Epilogue* | 109 |
| *Acknowledgements* | 112 |

IN THE ZEN TRADITION, a koan is a riddle that takes us to our deepest nature. Each chapter in this book opens with a koan. There is a purpose, to draw you into the present, and yet there is no purpose, for Zen is the tradition of no mind.

# PROLOGUE

*Nothing is exactly as it seems, nor is it otherwise.*
ALAN WATTS

LET US BEGIN this book with a moment of true silence. Not the kind of silence where your mind is racing with thoughts, but a deep, contemplative quiet. A silence that allows you to fully inhabit the present moment, to be fully here, now.

Do I have your attention? Are you *awakened*? To be awakened, or a *Buddha* (from the Sanskrit *budh*, meaning "to awaken," or "to become aware") is to be fully present, centered in the here and now, but with the benefit of wisdom and reflection. *That* is meditation. This book is about that wisdom and drawing you to the present—a good meditation.

*Zen,* a Japanese word borrowed from the Chinese *Chan,* borrowed from the Sanskrit *Dhyāna,* all mean meditation. This book is a meditation on the art of surgery—a meditation, in the deepest sense of the word, where you step back in the moment and really understand what's in front of you, the act of seeing what *is.* The act of stepping back, beyond habits, beyond preconceptions, beyond what we think we know, is a means of transcending the self. The stillness of mind created by meditation makes possible the examination of reality and, in this case, a different, if not deeper, understanding of surgery.

Surgery, like any art and life itself, is an expression of the soul, spiritual and deeply personal. Nothing special, and yet everything special. For those of us who are surgeons, lost in the daily routine, we sometimes lose sight of the beauty and wonder of what we do, but then we are reminded, from time to time, by outsiders or in moments of quiet contemplation, how special the art really is. Surgeons experience moments of great wonder and, yes, tranquility in the operating room. There is wisdom in the practice of surgery. It reveals to us our self, or lack thereof.

It is said in the Zen tradition that "When the student is ready, the teacher appears." That means a great deal, because not only must the student be ready to learn, but, at a larger level, there isn't necessarily a distinction between the *knower* and *knowledge*, there is just *knowing*, a unified process where the teacher and student become one. I have always felt it a great privilege to be able to teach students the art of surgery. This book is a collection of stories and lessons I have shared with surgeons I have trained over the years. It is a reflection on the art of surgery and what goes on and should go on in a surgeon's mind. My approach to teaching surgery was unconventional, drawing inspiration from various disciplines beyond the medical field. I often used props like Buddhist singing bowls, Native American talking sticks, and, my favorite, a *Magic 8 Ball* shaped like a giant eye, an unconventional tool that served as a playful and thought-provoking way of encouraging my trainees to take ownership of their learning and begin making independent decisions.

Koans, another teaching tool I frequently employed, are used in Zen to challenge the mind and stimulate enlightenment, often by presenting paradoxical or nonsensical questions. They are a way to break free from conventional thinking and discover deeper truths about oneself and the world. This book includes many koans for the reader to reflect upon and challenge what they think they know—about themselves, the practice of surgery, and the world around them.

In life, what you do often doesn't matter so much as how you do it, and what you think doesn't matter so much as why you think it. Any discipline, including surgery, trains the mind, in ways both good and sometimes bad. What follows here are meditations on the practice of surgery. They are not meant to be a path to perfection. There is no such thing as perfection, and yet, everything is perfect. They *are* meant, however, and like a good meditation, to make you pause and reflect, to look at how you practice surgery, and perhaps life, in another way.

# AWARENESS

*The more you know, the less you understand.*
LAO TZU

TO BECOME BETTER at anything, including surgery, we must be able and *willing* to examine ourselves, a self-awareness of our mind and actions. Distancing ourselves from habits, critiquing ourselves, and making improvements, as well as stepping back to reflect and see the bigger picture, comprise the examined life, both in *and outside* the operating room. If you can acknowledge what you don't know or what you aren't doing well without resenting or making excuses for it, your mind opens up to new ideas, and you might learn something, maybe even become a better surgeon.

Surgeons often begin their careers by emulating the styles of their mentors. This is understandable; it's a natural starting point. Reinventing the wheel is foolish, and avoiding unnecessary mistakes is prudent. By observing enough surgeries, you'll recognize distinct styles and schools of training, similar to the martial arts. Like any discipline, these styles come with their own traditions, pride, and ego.

Some surgeons adopt their training style as a foundation and build upon it, refining techniques, incorporating new advancements, and finding more efficient methods. Others, however, become overly reliant on what they learned early in their careers. This is a path to stagnation. The surgeon who fails to evolve beyond their initial style risks becoming outdated, unable to recognize a fundamental truth in surgery and life: the impermanence of *all* things.

Surgery, like life itself, is ever evolving. Only the surgeon who transcends the limitations of a fixed system can truly explore this truth and grow as a practitioner. This benefits both the surgeon and their patients. A truly dedicated surgeon has no fixed style. They operate based on the unique demands of each moment and the surgical field in front of them.

Throughout history, the establishment and insecure surgeons have notoriously resisted the evolution of surgical technique. This resistance reveals a deeper insecurity, an unwillingness to accept that only constant in life and surgery—change. Clinging to a creed, rejecting the new, and firmly sticking to a tradition provides the lesser surgeon with the illusion of stability, their comfort zone.

○

Two monks were arguing about a flag. One insisted, "The flag is moving." The other countered, "The wind is moving." They debated back and forth, unable to reach a consensus. And so a wiser monk stepped in and said, "It is not the flag that moves. It is not the wind that moves. It is your mind that moves…"

This Zen parable challenges the idea of absolute certainty and highlights how our perceptions and beliefs are often influenced by our own minds. It encourages humility and openness to different perspectives, reminding us that what we perceive as "right" might simply be a reflection of our own subjective viewpoint.

People commonly believe they are right and so are their actions. This is known as self-serving bias, a common human tendency with evolutionary roots. Confident individuals tend to thrive, and self-serving bias frequently accompanies confidence. This phenomenon is quite prevalent in the operating room. Surgeons readily claim credit for successes but are quick to blame external factors for failures. While this can bolster self-confidence, it doesn't necessarily contribute to better surgical skills. Self-serving bias can lead to overestimation of abilities, causing problems later on.

To counteract self-serving bias, surgeons must step back and objectively examine their work, meditating on outcomes and identifying both successes and failures. Discussing results with colleagues and exploring new techniques can also be beneficial. Humility is essential. By understanding oneself without emotional attachment, surgeons can identify their limitations. Recognizing what they don't know can open their minds to learning new things and discarding outdated practices. This allows for the expansion of skill sets and acknowledging the potential benefits of alternative surgical options, even if at first, they're not the ones providing them.

○

*The more you know, the less you understand.*[*] A koan is a story that teaches you a deeper truth about life, often by not knowing, or unlearning, something you think you know. One I often share with students goes like this: After a long morning and a lengthy turnover between cases, the attending (or senior) surgeon takes a break in the operating room lounge, a modern-day Zen temple. All he desires is a quiet cup of tea, but an overly eager junior surgeon interrupts. This surgeon doesn't just have questions; they have "ideas." Instead of listening, they blurt out one idea after another about how the case should be done. The attending listens patiently and begins pouring tea into the junior surgeon's cup. It's full, yet he continues pouring. The younger surgeon watches

---
[*] Lao Tzu. *Tao te Ching*.

respectfully until they can hold back no longer, exclaiming, "Stop! The cup is full. No more will go in!" To which the reply is, "Yes, and like this cup, you too are full of your own opinions. How can I teach you surgery unless you first empty your cup?"

Of course, I'm being a bit facetious here. It's expected that surgeons starting their careers have studied their cases, have ideas, and a surgical plan. This is part of the learning process. However, it's not uncommon for established surgeons to find themselves with a cup that's no longer empty. In surgery, emptying your cup means getting rid of self-delusions to view your practice, and perhaps life, from a different perspective. This requires a high degree of self-awareness, humility, and effort. You must analyze yourself, understand your style, preferences, habits, strengths, weaknesses, conceits, fears, and how past experiences or conditioning influence your surgical technique and decision making. Recognizing the limits of your ego is crucial. Only then can you transcend your style and experience to see the new, the unknown, and the unconventional. This is where you'll find truth and evolve as a surgeon.

In a way, you must die to all that you know. This is uncomfortable because it challenges the model of security we cling to. However, it's necessary for a better surgeon to emerge. In Zen or meditative practice, this is called beginner's mind—a mind without preferences or desires, one that sees things without bias, as if for the first time.

○

Do you take the time at the end of a case or the operating room day to reflect on your experiences? To consider what you might have done differently? Or is this not your habit at all? Does each completed case hold no meaning beyond its conclusion? Do you approach your life in a similar manner? Self-examination leads to self-awareness, and self-awareness leads to self-improvement.

We are all shaped by our experiences. These influence our worldview and reinforce what we think we know. For many, there's little room for something new. To see the world differently, it starts with examining ourselves—our experiences, habits, insecurities, delusions, what we don't see because our minds, like the cup, are full. Becoming a better surgeon starts and ends with you. *You alone are the path.*

# WU WEI

*The greatest carver does the least cutting.*

LAO TZU

CAN BRUCE LEE TEACH you anything about surgery? That, like anything else, depends on the individual being taught. *Enter the Dragon,* his last movie, opens with Lee having just pinned and tapped out his opponent. The scene changes. We find Lee in a monastery, on a lovely hill, branches swaying in the wind, birds singing in the background—all so very Zen—when Lee begins to wax philosophical.

**Shaolin Abbot:** I see your talents have gone beyond the mere physical level. Your skills are now at the point of spiritual insight. I have several questions. What is the highest technique you hope to achieve?

**Lee:** To have no technique.

**Shaolin Abbot:** Very good. What are your thoughts when facing an opponent?

**Lee:** There is no opponent.

**Shaolin Abbot:** And why is that?

**Lee:** Because the word "I" does not exist.

**Shaolin Abbot:** So, continue…

**Lee:** A good fight should be like a small play, but played seriously. A good martial artist does not become tense, but ready. Not thinking, yet not dreaming. Ready for whatever may come. When the opponent expands, I contract. When he contracts, I expand. And when there is an opportunity, I do not hit. It hits all by itself.

*Enter the Dragon* was a cultural phenomenon. Released shortly after Lee's untimely death, theaters were sold out everywhere. For many Westerners, it was their first introduction to Asian culture and philosophy. It ignited a martial arts phenomenon, with dojos opening everywhere and kung fu movies becoming a cinematic staple. Lee became a household legend.

Beyond its entertainment value, though, the film was a vehicle for Lee's philosophy on life and martial arts. Lee's observations about the mindset a martial artist must have when fighting apply to any human endeavor, including, and especially, surgery. Lee understood the intimate connection between mind, body, and action.* With this understanding, he achieved a level of mastery rarely paralleled in the physical arts.

Lee was a student of philosophy, particularly Taoism, the ancient Chinese tradition emphasizing living in harmony with the *Tao*.† The *Tao*, by definition, is indescribable, but can be thought of as the absolute harmony or energy that underlies and creates the universe. Some might call it God. Lee's phrase "not hitting" hints at one of Taoism's most

---

* The first two chapters of his book, *The Tao of Jeet Kune Do*, a martial art he invented, explore the interconnectedness of mind, body, and performance. Before delving into specific techniques, the book emphasizes the importance of this holistic approach. I often assigned this book to my surgical trainees who had fighting experience.

† The *Tao Te Ching*, a foundational Taoist text attributed to the sage Laozi from the 6th century BCE, explores the nature of the *Tao* (the Way). It emphasizes concepts like effortless action, *Wu Wei*, harmony with nature, simplicity, humility, and the interconnectedness of opposites. *Te Ching* (of Change)

important principles, *Wu Wei,* roughly translated as "non-doing" or "non-action," or paradoxically, the "action of non-action." It's a state of being where actions are effortless and in perfect harmony with the world.

True mastery requires not only skill but also the ability to step aside. Have you ever noticed how masters of any discipline seem to practice their art effortlessly, while amateurs struggle with excessive effort? That is *Wu Wei*. Lee developed Jeet Kune Do—a martial arts "style without style"—to reflect his understanding of *Wu Wei*. It's a response to the moment and the opponent, just as surgery should be—a response to the moment and the patient in front of you. *Just this.*[‡]

○

*See one, do one, teach one.*[§] In surgical training, junior surgeons spend a great deal of time observing their mentors operate before performing procedures themselves. When watching surgery, most young surgeons focus on the video monitor or the surgical

---
[‡] Koan
[§] Surgical Aphorism

field, concentrating on the anatomy and pathology. While this is important, observing a master surgeon's hands, like a pianist's or magician's, offers deeper insights. *Wu Wei.* Each movement is purposeful and efficient. Not a single step is wasted—perfect fluidity and economy of motion. Incisions are intentional, made with minimal pressure, cutting only the necessary tissue and using the most effective angles. The surgical field is accessed only when needed, as unnecessary movements waste time, and time in surgery is life, or at least a body part. Sutures are tied with the exact tension required to maintain wound apposition. The master surgeon selects only the essential maneuvers to achieve the desired anatomical outcome, without conscious thought—harmony born from simplicity.

*Simplicity.* I like to emphasize simplicity, or minimalism, in the operating room. It begins with the instruments you use. Some surgeons maintain egregiously large surgical trays, while others limit their trays to the essentials for the procedure at hand. When I started my surgical practice, I worked at a hospital where the surgical trays contained every instrument imaginable. Retrieving a needed instrument required searching through a table's worth of equipment, which was time-consuming. This was particularly problematic on weekends when I sometimes had inexperienced staff. When I moved to a new hospital and became head of the surgery service, I redesigned the surgical trays to include the minimum number of instruments. Additional instruments were kept in the room and opened only when necessary. This made things a lot simpler and quicker for everyone.

Novice surgeons often feel the need to keep and open every instrument they can access, seeking a sense of security "just in case" something goes wrong. As they gain experience, they become more confident in their abilities and can visualize exactly what they need to do. They may not empty out their trays entirely, but they begin to use fewer instruments to achieve the same outcome.

The concept of emptiness, or *sunyata*** in Zen and Indian philosophy, is central to understanding the importance of minimalism in both surgery and life.

---

** *Sunyata* is a Sanskrit term that translates to "emptiness" or "void" in English. In Buddhist and Indian philosophy, sunyata refers to the ultimate nature of reality, which is characterized by the absence of inherent self or substance, and from which all form emerges. It is often interpreted as a state of non-attachment and freedom from the illusion of a separate, permanent self.

Opening or holding onto unnecessary instruments only creates chaos, just as clinging to unnecessary ideas and possessions can clutter our minds and hinder our progress.

The operating room and the surgical field should be as empty as possible—like the surgeon's mind.

○

There is a Zen-like quality to a master surgeon's instrumentation and technique. In contrast, a beginning surgeon's actions may be forced. Cuts may be too deep or not deep enough. Angles may be unnatural, and the anatomical planes of the surgical field may be seen but not truly understood. That's understandable, experience is needed to developed expertise.

A master surgeon's actions are effortless, yielding like water. They are not driven by self or ego but are precisely what is needed in the moment. Fighting against instruments or the anatomy wastes energy and time. By softening and letting go, things unfold naturally. There is no instrument. By doing nothing, everything gets done. This is *Wu Wei*.

○

In surgery, the anatomy and not the surgeon must be respected. The surgeon merely alters the balance, doing as little as possible, while the body's remarkable self-healing powers do the rest. Subtle maneuvers performed at the right time may have a greater impact than complex ones, and certainly more impact than any maneuver done at the wrong time. The *Tao* reminds us that "only those who know when enough is enough ever have enough." Skilled surgeons understand this principle. We've all encountered cases where we wished we had stopped when things were going well. A slight misstep can lead to complications, such as nicking a vessel or the patient's inability to tolerate anesthesia.

There is wisdom in knowing when to stop—in a procedure, after a procedure, and, sometimes, before you even do the procedure—and that comes not just with experience, but with reflection and self-awareness. Human nature drives us do more and achieve perfection. And yet *perfection is an illusion*. In the mind's eye, there will always be "better."

When we impose our will on the world, we disrupt its harmony. The solution is not to not act, but rather to understand when and how to act in alignment with the natural flow of things. The foolish surgeon expends energy and time trying to do everything and achieves nothing. The wise surgeon does little but achieves much. This is creative quietude, the lesson of *Wu Wei* in surgery.

# UNCERTAINTY

*There is wisdom in the acceptance of uncertainty.*
SHERWIN NULAND

IF THERE'S ANYTHING certain, it's uncertainty. One of the most challenging concepts for young surgeons to grasp is uncertainty. Whether we call it loss of control, insecurity, impermanence, the unknown, or uncertainty—they all describe the same phenomenon. The only constant in life is change. Sound familiar?*

---

* I repeat this truism often in this book. Embracing it minimizes suffering. The Buddha described impermanence, or *Annitya (Sanskrit)*, as one of the two marks of existence. The other, *Anatta* or no-self, is the understanding that all things, including the self, are conditioned in a way that differs from how the human

This isn't unique to surgeons; as humans, we limit ourselves by our need for control and stability, which is essentially fear of uncertainty. We create explanations of the universe, religions, and unified theories to provide ourselves with the illusion of control, a security blanket in an uncertain world. Consider the decisions you've made in your life. Many were likely driven by a desire to mitigate uncertainty. Saving for a rainy day or locking the doors when leaving home are examples. While these are good habits now, they likely originated from a fear of unwanted or unknown outcomes. We may tell ourselves we're comfortable with change, but are we truly?

○

Physicians, however, *should* be comfortable with uncertainty. We all learned about it in medical school during our basic epidemiology and statistics courses. Remember p-values?

> P-value – the statistical probability of the occurrence of a given finding by chance

---

mind perceives them. Failure to accept these two fundamental truths leads to a unique type of human suffering known as *Dukkha*.

alone in comparison with the known distribution of possible findings, considering the kinds of data, the technique of analysis, and the number of observations

— Mosby's Medical Dictionary

P-values help physicians grapple with uncertain outcomes. They determine whether outcomes are due to chance or an actual intervention effect. Statistically significant p-values suggest a non-random, or actual, treatment effect. P-values quantify uncertainty and guide new practice paradigms in clinical studies. Physicians constantly reference p-values to shape their medical practices.

However, physicians may not fully appreciate the uncertainty inherent in p-values. The p-values guiding treatment decisions are often derived from homogeneous patient populations observed over fixed time intervals without confounding factors, unlike real-world medicine. The father of American medicine, William Osler, taught that no two patients with the same disease condition behave identically. Everyone is unique, with distinct genetic and environmental factors. Zen also teaches us that all phenomenon, patients included, are conditioned.

One might assume that physicians would critically analyze study results and determine their applicability to specific clinical situations. Unfortunately, this doesn't always happen. Drug companies and device manufacturers market evidence from trials conducted in patient populations that may not accurately represent real-world patients. This leads to a generation of physicians who treat patients based on these p-values, advocating the same study protocol for everyone due to their discomfort with real-world uncertainty. This is called scientific fundamentalism. And like religious and political fundamentalists who struggle with the uncertainty in the world around them, scientific fundamentalists cannot cope with the inherent uncertainty of medical practice. *There is wisdom in the acceptance of uncertainty.*

◯

*Great doubt, great awakening. Little doubt, little awakening. No doubt, no awakening.*[†] "Doubt" in the koan here is uncertainty. Surgeons should be comfortable with uncertainty, yet I've observed this is far from true. Insecure surgeons seek certainty,

---
[†] Koan

leading to predictable neuroses in the operating room. I frequently observe this in younger surgeons I've started to train, and unfortunately, sometimes in older ones as well. Surgeons uncomfortable with uncertainty rarely take risks in the operating room, which is where, under the watchful eye of a mentor or their own, they become better surgeons. Some, after years of avoiding uncertainty, become overly risk-averse, dissuading themselves and patients from reasonable procedures. Their skills stagnate, clinging to a limited range of procedures learned decades ago, arguing for mediocrity while their profession evolves around them. Hopefully, that isn't your surgeon. That's why we have surgical consent forms—to explain the risks, benefits, and alternatives of a procedure, as there's an inherent level of uncertainty involved in everything. That's life, and life is uncertain.

○

A truly skilled surgeon is not one who follows memorized surgical algorithms, although this can be helpful for beginners. Instead, they are able to navigate challenges and solve problems intraoperatively. Young surgeons may find it difficult to be comfortable with uncertainty initially, so I allow them to proceed with a procedure until they encounter difficulties. I then intervene or guide them through the steps to help them overcome the situation and develop valuable decision-making skills. Of course, patient safety and outcomes remain paramount, which is part of the art of teaching. I apply the same philosophy to my children. We all do, otherwise our children would never learn to make decisions for themselves. They need to become comfortable with uncertainty.

In surgery, and in medicine as a whole, there are multiple approaches to addressing the same problem. How comfortable are you with different approaches and with uncertainty? This is what makes us better surgeons. Do you fully engage with the case before you, or do you struggle to force it to conform to your expectations? The "right" way is not necessarily what someone else tells you or what you think it is, but what is appropriate for the moment—the specific case, your skill set, and your patient's needs. Every action has its place and time, everything ultimately fits together perfectly, and every movement arises from that perfection. In the Zen tradition, a koan is a puzzle that leads to a deeper level of truth. Every surgical case is a koan. Each one is unique and presents its own set of challenges. By being present in the moment, the answer always reveals itself—that, you can be certain of.

○

As human beings, we naturally seek security. Overcoming that requires a great deal of awareness. Yet, paradoxically, embracing uncertainty, rather than fearing it, can lead to inner strength and freedom, enabling you to navigate any situation, in life and in the operating room.

# STORIES

*It is a tale, told by an idiot,
full of sound and fury,
signifying nothing.*

WILLIAM SHAKESPEARE

THE PANDA HOLDS a special place in Chinese culture and history. Revered as a symbol of good luck, peace, friendship, and strength, it's often compared to the Taoist *yin-yang* symbol due to its contrasting black and white spots. Its calm demeanor embodies the peaceful harmony that can arise from balancing seemingly opposing forces.

Speaking of pandas, the movie *Kung Fu Panda* holds a special place in the hearts of many. More than just a beloved film that captivates audiences with its heartwarming characters, stunning animation, and thrilling action sequences, *Kung Fu Panda* offers a profound philosophical exploration that far exceeds what its title suggests. I've made it mandatory viewing for many of my surgical trainees. Those familiar with Eastern philosophy will recognize several familiar themes, including the importance of self-awareness, self-compassion, inner peace, and living in the present moment. The film masterfully develops these themes through the lens of an overweight, perpetually hungry, and sometimes self-critical panda, Po.

In one scene, Po, after a disappointing first day of training at the dojo, is walking home, drowning his sorrows in peaches. He contemplates giving up and returning to making noodles when he encounters the wise old tortoise, Oogway, the founder of kung fu and a Zen master. While you'll need to watch the movie to fully experience Po's angst, Oogway offers a bit of Zen wisdom: "Quit, don't quit. Noodles, don't noodles. You are too concerned with what was and what will be. There's a saying: Yesterday is history, tomorrow is a mystery but today is a gift. That is why it is called the present."

This brief moment encapsulates the experience of surgical training. Every surgeon has felt like Po at some point in their early careers. They have tried too hard and been less than compassionate with themselves. They can get lost in ruminating on past mistakes or future missteps, neglecting to make the most of the present moment. This internal narrative can become overwhelming. Unfortunately, some surgeons struggle with this more than others.

○

Humans are innately storytelling creatures, using narrative to shape their understanding of the world, their identities, and their place within it. This storytelling instinct is deeply ingrained within us and is why we reify reality with referents and labels, weaving a tapestry of meaning from the raw phenomenological material of our experiences.

As Zen philosophy reminds us, the mind is a powerful tool, capable of both enlightenment and delusion. Surgeons, like all humans, are prone to the mind's tendency to create stories, often through internal monologues. This phenomenon is frequently observed in the operating room, particularly among younger surgeons. It's understandable given the competitive upbringing and limited opportunities that many surgeons face. Their focus becomes so narrow that they see only the light at the end of that one tunnel, striving for the perceived standard of perfection modeled by their mentors.

However, it is important to remember that we are all human. Learning the art of surgery, like life, is a journey with its ups and downs.

Years ago, I mentored a brilliant, young surgeon who was hindered by her inner narrative. This was evident to anyone who worked with her. Hesitant during surgery, lacking trust in her skills and instincts, and clearly overthinking everything while listening to her own critical inner voice, her mind[*] had become her greatest adversary. Apparently, a previous mentor had yelled at her in the operating

---

[*] A student approached their teacher, the legendary monk and founder of Shaolin kung fu, Bodhidharma, and said, "My mind is restless." Bodhidharma replied, "Bring me your mind, and I will calm it." The student replied, "I've searched for my mind, but I cannot find it." Bodhidharma then said, "There, I have calmed it for you." The koan illustrates the elusive nature of the mind and the concept of *no self* or *Annata* in Zen and Buddhism.

room during a challenging case, damaging her self-confidence. Instead of forging her own narrative, she had adopted someone else's negative one. Her mindset was hindering her performance, and she was at a very real risk of not completing her training.

○

Learning surgery, like any other discipline, requires a focused approach. While the form may differ, and the stakes are higher, the underlying principles for acquiring expertise in surgery are generally the same, and mental training plays a crucial role. To train your mind, you must understand yourself. I often ask my students, children, acquaintances, and even myself odd and controversial questions to break down carefully constructed social and mental barriers. This allows for genuine connection and self-discovery. One question I frequently pose is, "What makes you, you?"[†] Nobody's ready for a question like that, and especially one that forces introspection and self-reflection.

---

[†] Koan

Tennis was one of the things that made this resident who she was. Well, if someone can overthink surgery, they can certainly overthink tennis. Anyone who plays the sport should read *The Inner Game of Tennis* by Timothy Gallwey. Gallwey, a tennis pro, understood how players' thoughts and attitudes can affect their performance. One line from the book summarizes the essence of sports psychology: "Every game is composed of two parts, an outer game and an inner game." The outer game is played against opponents, while the inner game takes place within the mind. Gallwey uses mindfulness, or being conscious of that inner narrative, to teach tennis players how to overcome their self-imposed limitations and unleash their full potential.

I've found that assigning young surgeons tasks unrelated to surgery, such as studying a skill like tennis, can be beneficial in teaching them about surgery through analogy. By watching *Kung Fu Panda* and reading about tennis and yoga, this surgeon began to change her mental narrative. To others, I've assigned a variety of materials, including books like *Sacred Hoops* and *Zen and the Art of Surfing*,

Sufi poetry, comic books, whatever is appropriate given the conditions at hand, to help them gain a new perspective. Some I have taken on field trips to the local planetarium, while others I have assigned a birding "big year,"[‡] informing them that I wouldn't graduate them without both their surgical logs and their bird list. These experiences were designed to draw them into the present moment and out of their minds. These examples of how overthinking can impact performance provided them with the necessary distance to observe their own thought patterns and how they influence their surgical practice. This awareness allowed them to overcome self-destructive thought patterns, develop a more positive mindset, and become better surgeons.

◯

Stories shape us. Consider how your favorite books or movies have influenced you. Our "self" is a collection of stories we identify with. Sometimes, it takes another story to help us view ourselves differently. Surgeons with impactful careers have

---

[‡] A term used in birding and other natural history pursuits, referring to a personal challenge to observe or document as many species as possible of a particular taxonomic group (e.g., birds, plants, mammals) within a given year, in this case their surgical training year.

taken responsibility for their actions and built their lives accordingly. They've overcome challenges by adopting the right mindset and rewriting their narratives. They understood, consciously or not, that by changing the stories we tell ourselves, we transform our lives.

# BREATH

*I talk to myself*
*'cause there is no one to talk to.*
*People ask me why,*
*why I do what I do.*
*They think that I'm crazy.*
*They say I'm strange,*
*'cause my attitude*
*has taken a change.*

CHRISTOPHER WILLIAMS

WE ALL TALK to ourselves. Of course, you do. We're almost always lost in thought, talking to ourselves, the little voice in our head telling us what to do—unless we've learned to silence it and be present without thinking. We live in a world of thoughts, and, from a very young age, we have been trained, like monkeys, to think in terms of words, symbols that refer to real things but aren't real things. You can think of a tree but that isn't really experiencing the tree. Rather, you're living a symbol, a virtual world in your mind, that passes as quickly as your mind verbalizes it. To really experience what you call a tree, you have to sit under its shade, smell its leaves, feel its bark—that's a tree and *that is life*.

The average person generates over 50,000 thoughts daily, most of which are pointless. Eastern traditions call this the "monkey mind." Our thoughts govern our actions, shaping our lives. Surgeons' minds are conditioned by years of competition, training, and self-judgment, influencing their thoughts and actions. Training surgeons involves observing how residents engage in internal dialogue. Words have a greater impact than you realize. If you're going to talk to yourself, you need to know what to say.

That's where we can take a lesson from hypnosis. Hypnosis isn't the sort of dramatic "trance" most people think it is. Rather, it's more like a deep meditation, one where the person being hypnotized is so relaxed that he or she is receptive to suggestion, and in that scenario it can be pretty effective.

In a hypnosis session, the hypnotized person is awake but just at the edge of sleep. It's at that time that our monkey mind and all the accompanying conscious cognition that interprets the world around us goes to sleep, and that's when you can make suggestions to someone, or their subconscious to be more precise, without having them be censured out. Stage hypnotists pick the most dramatic members of the audience to make suggestions to while therapeutic hypnotists put you in a comfortable chair and make suggestions that might help you do something meaningful, like losing weight or becoming a better public speaker. The concept is rather simple. The hypnotist, usually in their calm, monotonous voice, guides you into a relaxed state of mind, starting from deep breathing, to muscle relaxation, to, finally, that state just before sleep where the conscious mind is suspended. That's when the suggestions begin.

○

Breathing, specifically how you're breathing, is key to successful hypnosis. A subject's receptivity to suggestion and their calm state of mind can be assessed by observing their breathing patterns. Deep abdominal breathing, characterized by fewer breaths over a period of time due to fuller lung expansion, indicates receptivity. Chest breathing, associated with excitement or agitation, involves shorter breaths without abdominal expansion, indicating resistance.

Anyone with kids knows the practice of parental discipline, specifically the one-on-one dialogue after a misdeed. When a parent is agitated, they exhibit chest breathing, accompanied by pressured speech or yelling, and often engorged veins visible on their forehead. In that circumstance, the child instinctively mirrors the parent's physiology, including chest breathing, activating defense mechanisms and is unlikely to be receptive to any suggestion. Conversely, when the parent is breathing deeply and speaking calmly, the child is more likely to mirror the adult and be open to suggestion. In the latter circumstance, any discussion is more likely to have an impact. The same goes for any teacher-student relationship.

○

*The breath reveals the mind.*[*] By observing a surgeon's breath when he is operating, one can often anticipate their thoughts and when something bad might happen. A regular, relaxed breathing pattern suggests a surgeon isn't thinking too much about what they're doing but rather just doing it whereas a rapid breathing pattern indicates too much thinking, which never helps, and that's the time something will likely go wrong. The latter state of mind is often also accompanied by tremors, tachycardia, sweating, and, occasionally, the surgeon passing out. As the supervising surgeon at the table, I could deal with the latter scenario, but tremors are a real problem, and so is the poor decision-making that typically accompanies them. So right when I notice a change in their breathing pattern, I'll ask them to sit back and take a couple deep breaths. I'll make some suggestions, calmly—and I'm almost always belly breathing—and then have them return to the case. That's usually all that's needed. The tremors are better, and the case goes smoothly. There are surgeons who yell at their trainees in such circumstances, but that never helps and is almost always counterproductive.

---

[*] Koan

There's a scientific reason behind all of this, though I didn't grasp it until I had spent years meditating. Meditation made me a better teacher, in the lecture hall and in surgery. I used to think meditation was simply closing your eyes in a comfortable position while listening to peaceful music, but experienced meditators kept telling me there was more to it. My journey into meditation began with an eight-hour introductory course at the local Buddhist temple. It seemed like a good deal—*nirvana* for 30 bucks—but I should have paid more attention to the eight-hour part.

I arrived bright and early on a Saturday morning. After checking in, I was directed to a large, empty room where a monk instructed me to find a cushion to sit on and remain still. That was it for the formal instructions. I managed through the first couple of bathroom breaks, but after about three hours, I couldn't take it any longer. My mind wandered aimlessly from one subject to another. Forget inner peace; I needed to get out of there fast. The usual distractions I spent most of my life with were nowhere to be found. Instead, I was left with the miserable company of my own thoughts. So, right after the vegetarian lunch, I left. In fact, I went straight to Starbucks and to the movie theatre, back to modern society, and its nonstop hypnotic stimulation of the senses—a continuous mental orgasm without release. That was my first and, for a long time, last meditation experience. I returned to it a few years later and kept trying until I finally figured out what meditation was all about.

○

*The Universe opens and closes with each breath—let your mind rest there.*[†] Eastern philosophical and religious traditions have long recognized the importance of meditation and breathing. Inquire of any practitioner, and they will tell you why. And while approaches may vary, the underlying principle remains consistent: mindfulness of breath is key.

What is meditation? To answer this, we must first understand mindfulness. Mindfulness is being fully present in the here and now, free from thoughts of the past or future. It's silencing the "monkey mind." We occasionally experience peak moments of such presence, where thoughts cease, and we're fully

---
[†] Koan

immersed in the moment. This state, sometimes called *flow*, is a form of mindfulness. Through meditation practice, we can cultivate this state more frequently, even in less-than-ideal moments. In Zen, all moments hold equal importance.

However, most of the time, we find ourselves thinking about what's happening or, worse, something else. As a result, life and its offerings pass us by.

Meditation, at one level, is the practice of becoming more mindful through various forms of training, such as meditative breathing, chanting, yoga, tai chi, and others. At a deeper level, it is simply being present with what is, or being mindful, so that you can meditate wherever you are and whatever you are doing. For training surgeons, I prefer to teach meditative breathing as the method of practicing meditation since it is something you can return to in the operating room, clinic, or anywhere. You can't break out into a chant or a yoga pose in the operating room, but you always have your breath (when that's gone, I am fairly confident you won't need to worry about meditating, the monkey mind, or anything else). That's how I learned meditation—

first you master your body, then your breath, and then your mind follows.

The first step in meditation, which can be challenging for beginners, is stillness. Find a comfortable position and remain motionless. Mastering bodily awareness is essential, as it is in surgery. Patience with physical discomfort and the urge to move is crucial, as movement can distract the mind. These sensations are merely thoughts and perceptions. Many people don't wait long enough for them to subside. I recommend closing your eyes or using a blindfold at first to minimize distractions and focus on your breath.

Once you've mastered bodily stillness, the next step is to observe your breath. This slows down the mind. The mind can only hold one object at a time, making it easier to avoid getting lost in thoughts. Try to avoid labeling sounds, as labels themselves are thoughts. Focus solely on your breath. This directs your attention towards the object of breathing, away from random thoughts. New thoughts may arise, but recognizing them and returning to your breath creates a separation between you and those thoughts. By observing this, you can see how certain thoughts lead to emotional and physiological consequences. Thinking about something frightening or uncomfortable, like pain or a surgical mishap, can trigger a more rapid, chest breathing pattern, increased heart rate, and tension in your body, similar to what happens in the operating room. Conversely, thinking about something relaxing, like your last vacation or simply returning to your breath, can induce a deeper, belly-breathing pattern and a slower heart rate. With consistent practice, you become more present, develop greater detachment from your thoughts, and become less reactive to them.

Some people observe their breath, some chant, some count rosary beads (anxiety beads, really), some pray—it's all the same principle. They're all different ways to take you away from your thoughts and silence the mind. Begin with a few minutes of meditation and gradually increase the duration, practicing multiple times daily. Eventually, as your thoughts lose control over you, you'll cultivate a sense of inner calm—and some of the collateral benefits will include a more normal heart rate, lower blood pressure, improved digestion, and better sleep.

Why? *Yin and Yang.* The autonomic nervous system, responsible for non-voluntary activities like sweating, heart rate, and bowel movements, plays a crucial role. It consists of the *sympathetic* and *parasympathetic* divisions, which work in balance, much like yin and yang in Taoist philosophy. Yin and yang represent opposing but complementary forces, symbolizing the duality and interconnectedness of all things. Yin is often associated with feminine qualities like passivity, intuition, and receptivity, while yang is associated with masculine qualities like activity, logic, and assertiveness.

The sympathetic division, akin to yang, activates the body's stress response, increasing heart rate, blood pressure, and alertness, while slowing digestion. In stressful emergencies, where for example your ancestors were being chased by a saber tooth tiger on the savannahs of Africa, these would be very helpful in such a "fight or flight" response. This prepares the body for action by releasing neurotransmitters like adrenaline, epinephrine, and cortisol, which, relevant to our discussion here, can cause tremors and racing thoughts. Sympathomimetic drugs like caffeine have a similar effect.

The parasympathetic division, akin to yin, promotes relaxation and recovery, slowing heart rate, lowering blood pressure, and aiding digestion. The parasympathetic nervous system counteracts the sympathetic nervous system in non-stressful situations. Breathing patterns vary depending on which system is dominant. Shallow, rapid breaths indicate sympathetic dominance, while slow, deep breaths indicate parasympathetic dominance.[‡] Understanding this connection between breathing and physiological responses is key to understanding the beneficial effects of meditation.

Recall your anatomy class in medical school when you dissected the vagus nerve? This nerve, far more crucial than you might have ever imagined, is the key to your future well-being. The vagus nerve, the longest cranial nerve extending through the neck, thorax, and abdomen, is the lynchpin of the parasympathetic nervous system. Your vagal tone, or

---

[‡] In Zen and Vedic traditions, breath is a vital link between the body and mind. Deep, slow breathing is associated with a calmer, more focused state of consciousness. This aligns with the concept of "right mindfulness" in Zen, where attention is directed towards the present moment without judgment. In Vedic traditions, regulated breathing practices like Pranayama are employed to cultivate a deeper connection with the inner self. By slowing down the breath, one can quiet the mind and access deeper states of consciousness.

the activity of your vagus nerve, directly influences your overall health and stress levels. Higher vagal tone is associated with psychological and physical well-being, while lower vagal tone is linked to negativity, inflammation, and heart attacks.

Deep abdominal breathing, particularly with a long, slow exhalation, stimulates the vagus nerve and, consequently, the parasympathetic nervous system. Cold showers, yoga, and singing also activate the vagus nerve. The vagal response reduces heart rate, blood pressure, and improves brain function, promoting relaxation and digestion. Additionally, it releases anti-stress hormones like prolactin, acetylcholine, vasopressin, and oxytocin, which enhance memory, immune function, sleep, and reduce inflammation, allergic reactions, headaches, and pain. More importantly, it helps young surgeons perform with composure in the operating room, allowing them to think less and act more.

In essence, deep breathing means you're focused on the present moment, rather than dwelling on thoughts. By observing the breathing patterns of those around you, you can often discern their mental state. By cultivating a state of parasympathetic dominance through practices like meditation, individuals can improve their own well-being.

○

*When the mind is still, the universe speaks.*[§] In hypnosis, establishing a relaxed state and deep breathing is crucial. The phrasing of suggestions is equally important, especially in surgery where surgeons, like anyone else, engage in internal dialogue. If you can't control your internal dialogue, the words you use, or your neurolinguistic programming, become particularly relevant. Telling yourself not to have a complication can be counterproductive. New surgeons often fall into this trap, believing that avoiding negative thoughts will prevent negative outcomes. However, this strategy can have the opposite effect.

Neurolinguistic programming studies how self-talk influences outcomes. Skilled hypnotists are masters of neurolinguistic programming, phrasing suggestions effectively to elicit desired subconscious responses. Positive phrasing is crucial because the subconscious doesn't hear "no's." This principle, the

---
[§] Koan

power of positive phrasing, is as crucial in surgery as it is in hypnosis or any other field. Telling yourself not to have a complication is akin to telling yourself to have one. You might as well have been saying "Have a complication. Have a complication. Have a complication..." because that's exactly what your subconscious hears, leading to self-hypnosis and a self-fulfilling prophecy.** Consider this. If you're playing basketball and taking the game winning shot, you're better off telling yourself its going in, because the minute you start thinking about how not to miss it, you're probably going to miss it.

○

For the beginning surgeon, focusing on both physical technique and mental state can be challenging, especially when outcomes are at stake. A mentor who can provide guidance and support is invaluable.

Learning surgery, like any discipline, involves training the mind. Surgery, like any physical or performance art, and life itself, is primarily mental.

---

** That's not to say visualizing and training for managing potential complications is wrong, but not during the case at hand. That should be done ahead of time, like on a surgical simulator.

Talent alone is insufficient; mastering the mind is crucial for becoming a skilled surgeon. The best surgeons use their minds as tools.

Pay attention to your self-talk, breathe deeply, and practice regularly. By cultivating a calm and focused mind, you become a master surgeon.

# POSTURE

*The most important things in our practice are our physical posture and our way of breathing.*

SHUNRYU SUZUKI

ONE OF MY pet peeves is posture. Why? Well, it's a reflection of deeper issues, a shadow aspect of my psyche. I struggled with poor posture for much of my life, and still do at times, so I'm particularly sensitive to it in my students and children. I established a requirement with all the surgeons I've trained: they must have good posture to graduate. Schools no longer teach posture, and modern lifestyles involve prolonged periods of hunching over keyboards, phones, or steering wheels. Poor posture becomes a habit, difficult to break, and can even be seen as a karmic curse.

Surgeons often have poor posture, which is understandable given the demands of their profession. They spend long hours standing in the operating room and, when not performing procedures or examining patients, are hunched over computers. Traditional surgical techniques require surgeons to stand at the bedside, with their heads down or craned forward for those using microscopes. This posture, with contracted arms and shoulders, is detrimental to physical health.

Poor posture not only looks bad but can also lead to significant health problems. Each inch of head forward posture increases the weight on the spine by ten pounds. A few inches can add thirty to forty pounds of pressure, causing head and neck pain. Additionally, poor posture affects breathing and reduces lung capacity. More importantly, it can shorten careers. I lecture all my trainees on posture and remind them frequently during surgery and clinic visits to stand straight and tall. I even threatened to not graduate one of my fellows until they corrected their posture.

○

The concept of the "superior man" (*junzi*) and the "inferior man" (*xiaoren*) is a recurring theme in the *I Ching*, also known as the *Book of Changes*. This ancient Chinese divination text provides guidance on personal, philosophical, and political questions through a system of hexagrams. In hexagrams like 15 (on modesty) and 33 (on retreat), the superior man is described as acting with integrity, confidence, and wisdom, contrasting the timidity and hesitation of the inferior man.

An *I Ching* diviner I once met elaborated on this concept. They explained to me that the superior man enters a room with confidence, stands with poise, and speaks with authority. In contrast, the inferior man enters timidly, slouched and hesitant. Even with knowledge and expertise, their demeanor undermines their credibility. This phenomenon is likely familiar to you.

Imagine yourself as a patient waiting on an exam table. Your surgeon enters the room, slouching rather than walking confidently. They avoid eye contact and hesitate during their diagnosis and treatment recommendations. Despite their technical skills, their demeanor raises doubts, and your subconscious sends warning signals. Conversely, many charlatans have excellent posture, understanding, consciously or subconsciously, the importance of appearances. How you stand and compose yourself affects how others perceive you. More importantly, your posture affects your self-perception and confidence. Good posture can boost self-esteem, while poor posture can hinder it.

○

*When you sit, sit. When you stand, stand. When you walk, walk. Don't wobble.*\* I wobbled. After a decade of surgical practice, my posture had deteriorated to such an extent that I felt like I had wound back the evolutionary clock several million years. Determined to improve my posture, I sought the help of a rehabilitation therapist. For several months, I diligently worked out and stretched the muscles needed to stand with dignity. While these exercises were beneficial, I found that a posture-correcting

---

\* This koan highlights the Zen principle of being fully present and mindful in whatever posture or activity you are engaged in. It encourages stability and focus in both body and mind.

shirt was even more effective. The shirt, with strategically placed elastic bands, retracted my shoulders and helped me stand up straight. Although uncomfortable to wear, the shirt made me acutely aware of my posture throughout the day. This awareness, more than the shirt itself, was the key to improving my posture. You have to be aware of your posture to have good posture.

*Zen, too, is all about awareness.* Shinryu Suzuki, a Zen Buddhist monk, is credited with introducing Zen to America. His book, *Zen Mind, Beginner's Mind*, is a popular guide to Zen practice. While it may initially seem perplexing, especially for those easily distracted, repeated readings offer valuable insights into the meditative mindset that should permeate all aspects of life, including surgery.

In Zen, self-awareness is paramount. By recognizing your thoughts and behaviors, you can shed habitual patterns and focus on the essence of your actions, whether it's laundry, basketball, or surgery, all equally important, well maybe the latter a little more so. This is what Zen practitioners call "practice." According to Suzuki, physical posture and breathing are essential components of practice.

Similarly, in surgery, posture affects everything, from mindset to breathing and physical health, and operating itself. Maintaining good posture requires constant awareness. By practice, and being mindful of your posture, you can improve your overall well-being and performance.

○

*The body is the temple of the mind.*[†] How you stand, breathe, and think significantly impacts your performance, not only in the operating room but in all aspects of life. Stand tall, breathe deeply, and be mindful of your thoughts. These are the foundations of a successful and fulfilling surgical career and life.

---

[†] Koan

# KARMA

*Wherever a dog walks his tail must follow.*
ZEN PROVERB

Some days, fate seems inevitable. During my surgical training at Stanford, I often assisted the department chair. One such day, everything seemed to go wrong. The room turnover was slow, medications were delayed, and the anesthesiologist was nowhere to be found. We were running two hours behind schedule. The head honcho looked at me and said, "Saad, this is surgical karma."

"Surgical karma?" I asked.

"Yes, indeed," he replied. Apparently, surgical karma refers those days when everything seems to go wrong, despite your best efforts. Many people associate karma with fatalism, believing that bad luck is predetermined. However, karma is simply the law of consequence. Every action, whether in the operating room or in life, has a corresponding result, even if it manifests years later. *Choices have consequences. Nothing is random.*

○

People complain about things that *happen* to them. It's easier to blame fate or external forces than to accept responsibility for your own actions. By examining events in detail, we can often trace the outcome back to *a decision we made.* This understanding is essential for becoming a good surgeon. The best surgeons accept responsibility for outcomes, especially when they're not optimal. Self-awareness is crucial for personal growth and success. They thoroughly investigate the chain of events, identifying errors in logic and technique, areas for improvement, and bad habits. This is a continuous process that leads to ongoing improvement. Karma isn't destiny. Success or failure is a result of choices and actions, not chance or fate.

Think of basketball. When a shot is missed, do you simply take another one or analyze the reasons for the miss? Were your feet positioned correctly? Did you apply enough lift? Was your elbow tucked in? Did you follow through? Did you aim for the center of the rim? Adjust. Get better. That's karma—choices and actions, not chance or fate, produce outcomes. This applies to all aspects of life, including surgery.

○

*Scratch before you itch.*\* Think about it. What does it mean? It's a classic teaching koan I like to pose to my students and kids. Got it? Well, it's probably not what you think it is. Or maybe it is. Who knows? Only you can answer that.

Anything, words included, can mean anything to anyone. Words especially—they're just symbols for reality, not reality itself. For me, it's quite simple. Often, when you have an itch somewhere, you

---

\* One of my favorite Zen koans, illustrating the principle of anticipatory action and mindfulness in surgery.

scratch it without even realizing you did. We're talking about reflexes and habits here, things you're not even thinking about.

The itch triggers a reflex, a scratch for the purpose of this koan, but really any other reflex or habit you might have, like your thought patterns. You feel an itch and, most of the time, you're not mentally there. You've already scratched it. You might not even know you're doing it unless someone points it out to you. It's like when you rub your eye—no one seems to ever rub their eye, but they all do.

I'm sure you thought about it the first time you ever had an itch, but that was a long, long time ago. Now it's all reflex. Well, the next time you have an itch, see if you can catch yourself. That's awareness. Don't scratch—or *decide* to scratch. Whatever the case, you're awakened, conscious, and present. You had to think about it. You're responding, not reacting.

If you think about the koan long enough, you're not thinking about anything else, and you might see how your mind works. That's the deeper value of studying koans. The koan's value lies in its ability to redirect your focus. By pondering it deeply, you can gain insights into your own thought patterns. For surgeons, this self-awareness can be transformative. Many actions, from everyday habits to surgical techniques, are performed reflexively. While these actions may not be inherently wrong, examining them can reveal areas for improvement.

Breaking habits requires conscious effort. You must "scratch before you itch," meaning you must be mindful and present to break free from ingrained patterns. This takes mental energy and work. Otherwise, you may become a prisoner of your habits. A study on smokers found that the arm's reach for a cigarette often precedes the desire for one, illustrating how habits can operate on a subconscious level.

○

Our choices shape our actions, which become habits, which in turn define us. The human brain is programmed to repeat actions. Neural networks, the chains of neurons that encode our actions, strengthen with repetition. When we perform an action for the first time, we create a neural pathway. Repeating the action reinforces this pathway, increasing the number of neurotransmitters released and receptors expressed between neurons. This neural network becomes solidified, requiring less energy to activate. As a result, our thoughts and actions become habitual, seemingly effortless. This established pathway becomes the path of least resistance, making it easier to repeat the same behaviors. However, this can also lead to predictable patterns of behavior. That's why we always think and act the way we do, predictably.

Understanding how habits are formed allows us to rewire our neural pathways. Through insight, meditation, and self-awareness, we can break old habits and create new habits that lead to personal growth and professional development.

There are no accidents. Who we see in the mirror is a reflection of our choices. Our actions today shape who we will be tomorrow. This understanding, rooted in the concept of karma, emphasizes the interconnectedness of our actions and their consequences. Our choices today shape who we become tomorrow.

# MISTAKES

*Water which is too pure has no fish.*
HONG ZICHENG

THE BIGGEST MISTAKE you could possibly make is to assume mistakes won't happen. Everyone, and I mean everyone, makes mistakes. I make tons of them. Just ask my kids. To them, everything I do is a mistake. It's a part of learning and growing up. Mistakes, experience, and expertise go hand in hand. A good mistake is good Zen. It's like a koan, an opportunity for deeper understanding, both in life and in surgery. Good surgeons know this well. But learning to learn from your mistakes is not easy, and one of the key components in getting surgeons to be better is changing their attitude toward mistakes. Mistakes aren't obstacles in your path—they *are* the path.

Surgeons who are just starting out in their careers hate making mistakes. Somehow, they've convinced themselves that mistakes shouldn't happen. It's the first thought process I try to change. Shit happens. That's life. You have to deal with it. It's a simple philosophy. Instead of perseverating on a mistake, reflect on it, learn something, come back the next time, and do whatever you were doing better. There's no excuse for the mistakes that come from being neglectful or unprepared, but beyond those it can reasonably be assumed that mistakes will happen in the operating room. Part of being a teacher is not allowing students to make critical mistakes that lead to bad outcomes, and another part of being is allowing students the freedom to make mistakes that lead to experience. You have to be able to make mistakes and deal with them so that later on, when you're on your own, you can deal with problems. That's the zen of teaching surgery—allowing students to make mistakes, without making mistakes. I've seen sur-geons yell at their juniors and staff when a mistake is made, and that's never helpful. It just tells me that the surgeon hasn't figured out mistakes happen and, instead of doing the hard work to investigate and learn from them, they've developed a terrible habit of compensating by blaming others. It's particularly unfortunate when someone like that is teaching because they're going to model a generation of sur-geons after themselves.

Typically, when a beginning surgeon makes a mistake, and certainly when he or she is yelled at, two things happen. They're not comfortable with the concept that mistakes are a learning tool so they either deny they ever made one or they set off a monolog in their head about how terrible they are for making the mistake. At that point, someone, like me, must change the narrative, making sure they recognize what's happening, so that they can distance themselves from the internal dialog, take responsibility for their actions, and learn something from the experience. It's important not to dwell on the mistake. You can't change what happened, but you can change how you respond to it.

Sensitivity to criticism can be a common issue in operating rooms, particularly for junior surgeons. While it's understandable that some surgeons may be bothered by yelling or harsh words, it's important to recognize that the real problem often lies in our own perceptions and thoughts about the situation. The key to overcoming this is to understand that the only real solution is to distance yourself from your thoughts. Your thoughts about things are almost always the real problem, and many of those thoughts are far worse than whatever is being said.

○

I have guided many of my residents through a meditation practice to get them to understand that if they don't distance themselves from the thoughts in their head, serious emotional and psychological consequences ensue, leading to bad habits and poor self-confidence. I have them sit quietly somewhere and relive the experience. When they do, their heart rate picks up, they start breathing quickly, it gets tough to focus and stay calm, and some develop physical tension somewhere in their body. That's stress. I want them to see and feel that response. But then I have them step out of that experience so that they can see how one bad memory or thought can lead to a train of others, and that those thoughts are accompanied by physiologic and mental changes. If you can add some mental distance, and you can do it long enough, the experience and your pondering over it won't have the same negative effect on you. You can apply the technique to any event, mistake or not, in the operating room or elsewhere, which still carries an emotional burden for you.

○

In Zen, there is no good or bad. There is only what *is*. Your judgment makes something good or bad. Everything has only the value that you apply to it. That's what "emptiness" in Zen is all about. It's not that things are empty or have no value, it's just that they have only the value that you or someone else attributes to them. That much you know from personal experience. There are things that mean the world to you, like your favorite operating room stool, your opinions, your personal beliefs, but the same things mean absolutely nothing to someone else. All of that has to do with your conditioning – how you've been brought up, where you've lived, your education, your cultural background, your genes, etc. Society and your parents have a lot to do with that conditioning.

Well, you can forget all of that in surgery. In surgery, there *is* good and bad. You can tell who's a good surgeon by their attitude toward mistakes. What do you do when you make a mistake? When anyone makes a mistake? When something doesn't go as planned? Do you blame someone else, anyone else, or do you accept responsibility for what happened? A good surgeon assumes responsibility for every mistake—his *and* everyone else's. Why? Because in the end, he realizes it's the mistake that counts, and its consequences on the patient, not who made it. When you think that way, you'll take the time to find out what went wrong and why, and then you'll know how to make sure it never happens again. Analyzing mistakes is a means of self-awareness and self-reflection, and self-reflection leads to self-improvement and, in this case, a better surgeon. It's not easy. It takes all sorts of fortitude, mental and otherwise, to hold yourself accountable. On the other hand, the bad surgeon will always find someone else to blame mistakes on, forgetting whatever happened as fast as they possibly can. It's the easy way out. There's no mental anguish that way. That mentality, very quickly, becomes a habit, a really bad one.

To make a good mistake, you have to first make a decision. Decision making is critical to being a good surgeon. Decisions reflect how an individual deals with uncertainty. Individuals who are comfortable with uncertainty make decisions with the attitude that they'll learn something from the consequences of their actions, even if it's a mistake. They've figured it out. Nothing in life is certain. The only certainty is uncertainty. Then there are those who would rather not make decisions because they live in fear of the anticipated consequences. Those are the students we dread as mentors. You can tell who these individuals are. They typically take too long to make a decision and almost always make the wrong one, over and over again. You either know or you don't know. And if you don't know, hand over the case to someone who does, look it up, or learn from your mistakes. Now you know. It's important to recognize if you're the type who can't make decisions easily so you can change your habits and way of thinking. You go nowhere in surgery, or life, if you can't make decisions, and if you can't make them quickly. Things fall apart if you take too long to make a decision. In surgery, sometimes it's better to deal with the consequences of a bad decision than to hesitate or not make a decision at all.

And so, there are two types of bad surgeons. The first are those who can't make decisions, and the second are those who don't learn from their mistakes. Sometimes you get both in the same person. My chairman at Stanford once told me that you have to make a good decision the first time; otherwise, you'll have to make many more decisions to make up for it later. That's true. That comment has stuck with me for the longest time, and after twenty years of operating it carries a slightly different meaning for me. I used to take it as a critique on not making bad decisions, but it's really just a statement of fact. You're not always going to make a good decision the first time. There are clearly some stupid decisions. You learn about those in books. Those are the kind you avoid. Beyond those, the only bad decisions are the ones you make a second time. That's a sign you weren't paying attention, and you weren't with it mentally enough to learn from the first time you screwed up. Hopefully, when you make a mistake, someone points it out to you, or you take the time to reflect on it, so that the experience makes you a better surgeon the next time around.

○

Mistakes are koans. They're teaching tools with great insight. When you're wrong, you're actually right. When you make a mistake, and you can figure out why, and know how to prevent it from happening again, you're right. They can be a path to self-realization. They teach you something new and help you give up something old. When a mistake happens, it should be cherished as it brings us closer to the art, making us better surgeons and healers. Sometimes making a mistake is the best thing that could have ever happened. That all depends on you.

# INTERDEPENDENCE

*In a snowfall that covers the winter grass,
a white heron uses his own whiteness to disappear.*

DŌGEN

IN HINDU MYTHOLOGY, the world originated from the will of the primordial cosmic energy, *Shakti*. *Shakti* transforms into life as we know it, ultimately returning to *Shakti*. This creative process is called *Lila*, the divine sport. Life is a game, and the world is its playing field. However, under the illusion or magic spell of *Maya* (our egos and the perceived phenomenological world around us), humans forget their divine nature and the interconnectedness of all life, and it is because we forget we suffer.

I appreciate this myth not only for its universal message but also for its perspective on life as a game. If life in its many forms is a game, you can learn to play it well. Work, family, love, your hobbies – it's all life, and it's all a game. How you play one form is how you play the whole. Lessons from one apply to the others. The art of surgery is one of those many forms, one where life, or at minimum a body part, hangs in the balance. Surgery is a divine sport and, more importantly, a team sport.

Every living thing is interdependent. It depends on something else. We cannot achieve anything alone. You're here because someone, a lot of some–ones, got you here. Even the simplest actions are conditioned by the actions of countless individuals. It's true in life, and it's true in the operating room. That patient on the table, under your knife, didn't just get there. Someone brought him in that morning, someone admitted him to the hospital, someone got him dressed, someone set up his intravenous lines, someone in the room helped move him to the table, someone administered anesthesia, someone will take him home. There were a lot of "someones." Medicine, especially surgery, is a team sport, and successful surgeons understand this.

○

Buckminster Fuller was an American architect, inventor, and futurist. He is best known for his geodesic domes and his theories on *synergy*. His concept of synergy posits that the whole is greater than the sum of its parts, and that this emergent intelligence is greater than the sum of the individual intelligences of the system's components. Fuller believed that humanity could overcome its problems and create a sustainable future through cooperation and collaboration.

The power of synergy in biological systems is evident in the human body. The human brain is a complex network of neurons that work together to produce consciousness, thought, and emotion. This emergent intelligence is greater than the sum of the individual neurons. For example, while each neuron is capable of simple electrical signals, the brain as a whole can perform complex tasks like recognizing faces, understanding language, and solving problems.

Synergy also offers a valuable lens through which to view the operating room environment. In the operating room, this means that the team's collective effort and cooperation produce a better outcome than any individual could achieve alone.

Consider a surgical team performing a complex procedure. The surgeon, anesthesiologist, nurses, and technicians all have specialized roles. When working together effectively, they create a synergistic environment where the whole is greater than the sum of its parts. The surgeon provides the overall leadership and technical expertise. The anesthesiologist ensures the patient's safety and comfort during the procedure. The nurses assist the surgeon and maintain a sterile environment. The technicians operate the medical equipment.

When each team member performs their role effectively and communicates clearly with others, the procedure is more likely to be successful and have a positive outcome. This is an example of synergy in action. This is why effective leadership, communication, and teamwork are essential in the operating room.

Although everyone plays a role in the operating room, the surgeon is ultimately responsible for the outcome. Training surgeons involves teaching them this concept, that they have to develop a leadership mindset.

Surgery is a high-stakes game where winning matters. In the operating room, every detail matters. From the instruments used to the team's dynamics, each element contributes to the outcome. Effective leadership in the operating room requires preparation, confidence, delegation skills, and accountability. Anticipating instruments and medications, maintaining confidence, delegating tasks effectively, and providing clear directions are essential. When things go wrong, taking responsibility is crucial, even if it's not your fault.

I've found that a successful approach is to attribute team credit for positive outcomes but take personal responsibility for negative ones. This mindset encourages problem-solving and continuous improvement, and by understanding the concept of synergy, surgeons can foster a more collaborative and effective team environment, ultimately leading to better patient outcomes.

○

*The ten thousand things are one.*\* A surgeon grows to lead in the operating room. Whether it's a routine case or a complicated one, there comes a moment of introspection when the young surgeon sees himself as the leader of the team. He realizes that everyone has a crucial role for which he is responsible. In that moment, he understands the interdependence of the team and his role within it. That is the moment he is transformed. Nothing is ever the same again.

---

\* Koan

# ABSOLUTION

*If you can fill the unforgiving minute with sixty seconds' worth of distance run . . .*

RUDYARD KIPLING

ALL OF US have experienced the unforgiving minute—the moment we wish never happened, the one that lingers in our memory forever and we would do anything to take back. In life, it's how you respond to that unforgiving minute that makes all the difference.

Surgeons, like all healthcare professionals, face complications. These unexpected events can occur despite our best efforts and extensive knowledge. We discuss the risks and benefits of surgery with our patients, including the possibility of complications. However, when a complication occurs, it takes on a personal significance for both the patient and surgeon.

Surgeons often relive complications for years, even if they occurred in the far past. Learning from these experiences is crucial for growth and development. Life and a surgeon's maturation are defined by one's response to adversity.

When faced with adversity, it's challenging to maintain an open mind. Bad surgical experiences, without wisdom and compassion, can breed fear. Fear is a powerful motivator, but it can also be paralyzing, especially for surgeons. While fear can keep us on our toes, excessive fear can hinder performance.

After negative experiences, surgeons may become overly self-critical. This can lead to a downward spiral, affecting future performance and potentially jeopardizing their careers. However, with wisdom and self-compassion, surgeons can overcome these challenges. By understanding the root causes of errors and learning from them, surgeons can improve their skills and prevent future complications.

By investigating what happened and why, without getting emotionally involved, you can learn from the experience and become a better surgeon. Mindfulness techniques, such as meditation and controlled breathing, can be helpful if the event is still emotionally distressing. A mentor, colleague, or psychologist can also provide guidance and support.

Doubt can be contagious, spreading from the mind to the sinews. It's crucial to address doubt proactively. While a run of good luck can boost confidence, complacency can lead to future problems. Mind–fulness can transform a negative experience into a positive one, while its absence can turn a positive experience into a disaster.

Adversity builds character. The true measure of a surgeon is their response to challenges, especially in that "unforgiving minute." Difficult moments will inevitably arise. Things will go bad at some point. That you can count on. And when that happens can you keep your emotions and thoughts at bay and focus and deal with what's in front of you, in surgery and afterwards, in the best interest of your patient, and in your best interest as well? That's the question that needs to be answered. It's the only way you can honor the moment, the experience, and, most importantly, the patient. All you can do is fill every minute, but especially the unforgiving ones, all sixty seconds, with as much effort, wisdom, and compassion as you can. If you can do that, in surgery and in life, then, to finish off Kipling's verse, "yours is the earth and everything that's in, and—which is more—you'll be a man, my son."

# INTUITION

*The word is not the thing.*
*The description is not the described.*
*The word mountain is not the mountain.*
*The description of the mountain is not the mountain.*

JIDDU KRISHNAMURTHI

THE ART OF SURGERY, with its intimate exposure to the human body, offers a unique perspective on the nature of medicine. Yet, the constant barrage of labels and categories that accompany the study of surgery can obscure the underlying beauty and mystery of the human body.

In medicine, there are countless labels. Thousands of disease conditions are named after individuals (eponyms) or have specific scientific names. The human body has thousands of named structures. Every drug has a chemical name, a generic name, and multiple brand names. There are names for surgical procedures, diagnostic tests, and therapies. Each specialty has its own set of terminology, a language specific to their field. For a seasoned surgeon, the number of terms could easily reach into the hundreds of thousands. This tyranny of words can limit our perception and prevent us from accessing the unspoken world from which creativity and intuition flow.

○

*The five colors blind the eye. The five tones deafen the ear. The five flavors dull the taste.* This line from the *Tao te Ching* reminds us how labels limit our perception of reality. The real world is more "colorful" than the range of colors we afford it and thus reify it with. On the other hand, the "Unspoken World,"[*] as Zen

---

[*] Alfred Korzybski, engineer and philosopher, developed the theory of General Semantics which emphasized the importance of language and thought in shaping our perception of reality. Korzybski coined the term "Unspeakable World" to refer to the aspects of reality that cannot be fully captured or

philosopher Alan Watts described it, is a realm beyond the limitations of language and thought. It is a place of intuition, creativity, and connection. It is reality itself, without the referent of language. By stepping outside the confines of labels and categories, surgeons can tap into this realm and gain a deeper understanding of their patients and the mysteries of the human body.

The use of labels and categories, while helpful for understanding and treating diseases, creates an illusion of reality. By reducing complex biological processes to simple terms, we risk losing sight of the underlying interconnectedness and wonder of the human body. Once we've given something a name, we no longer see it the way we did the first time, with a beginner's eye, but rather we just see the label.[†‡]

○

---

expressed through language. Alan Watts later adopted and expanded upon this concept, using the term "Unspoken World" in his own philosophical explorations.

[‡] There is a Zen teaching story where a child describes a colorful creature singing beautifully in a tree and asks her father what it is. When he tells her it is a bird, she will never see the bird the same way again, with the beginner's eye. This mirrors our earlier discussion of the beginner's mind, a mind free from preferences and desires, objective and without bias.

A few years ago, a surgical fellow, brimming with excessive energy, presented her first case to me in clinic. She described every detail and nuance of the anatomy with vivid clarity, and yet clearly searching for a label. Of course, as physicians we often know the diagnosis right away from years of experience and pattern recognition, but I told her we would take several minutes to pause and reflect before I gave her the answer, a de facto funereal moment of silence. Why? Because that would be the last time she would ever see that disease in the same way.

○

As surgeons, we are heavily invested in a specific learning style, known as *auditory-digital*. This style involves labeling and reasoning things out to learn, in contrast to *visual*, *auditory*, and *kinesthetic* (movement) modalities of learning which are less verbal. While this approach can be helpful, it can also limit our ability to access the unspoken world of our intuition. By cultivating mindfulness, we can balance our auditory-digital learning style with a more intuitive approach.

Intuition, often overlooked in the modern medical world, is a powerful tool for surgeons. It is a subtle awareness that can guide us beyond the limitations of labels and categories. By cultivating our intuition, we can access a deeper level of understanding and make more informed decisions.

A surgeon's intuition is built over time through a combination of experience, mindfulness, team collaboration, and learning from past cases. While data and evidence remain critical in decision-making, intuition plays a key role in recognizing subtle patterns that may not be immediately obvious through analytics alone. By refining their ability to tap into this subconscious awareness, surgeons can become more adaptive and effective in the operating room.

Intuition in surgery is the ability to make quick, effective decisions based on experience, pattern recognition, and subtle cues that are difficult to articulate but vital for surgical outcomes. Repetition and exposure build experience, allowing our brains to recognize patterns faster and make decisions quicker subconsciously. After surgeries, reflecting on difficult cases, what went well or didn't, sharpens intuition for future scenarios. This internalization of experience helps with quicker, more accurate assessments.

The practice of silence can be a powerful tool for accessing intuition. By quieting the mind and turning inward, we can create space for intuition and creativity to emerge. In the operating room, the silence that precedes a procedure can be a moment of deep connection with the patient and the underlying forces at play.

Surgeons who practice mindfulness techniques (such as deep breathing or staying focused on the task) often find they can better "hear" their intuition. When attention is fully on the surgery, they may be more attuned to subtle cues that indicate whether something is going right or wrong, a "gut feeling" during procedures, where something feels "off" despite all technical indicators suggesting normality. Being in tune with these subtle sensations can be crucial in preventing complications.

While surgical decisions are rooted in evidence-based practice, there are moments when data alone cannot provide all the answers. Learning to trust the subconscious mind, especially after years of experience, allows for a blend of analytic and intuitive decision-making. Engaging in simulations, challenging cases during training, and attending surgical case conferences can enhance a surgeon's intuitive responses. Discussing cases with colleagues and receiving feedback after procedures help refine a surgeon's ability to tap into their intuition. This process allows them to compare their personal experiences with others' perspectives, reinforcing certain instincts while challenging others. These practices help develop the "muscle memory" and "mental memory" that surgeons rely on.

In high-stress environments like the operating room, it's easy for a surgeon to ignore their intuition if they are overwhelmed by too much data, or what's known as "cognitive overload." Learning to focus on what's important and managing stress through meditation, breaks, or relaxation techniques can help surgeons become more attuned to their intuitive insights. Surgeons can train themselves to distinguish between intuition and cognitive biases (e.g., confirmation bias). By being aware of these biases, they can prevent them from clouding their judgment while still listening to their intuitive responses. We've also already spoken of the need to stay curious, in seeking new information and improving one's knowledge base, and in stepping out of one's comfort zone in trying new techniques, and these novel challenges all help to broaden the intuitive skillset.

A surgeon's intuition is built over time through a combination of experience, mindfulness, collaboration, and learning from past cases. While data and evidence remain critical in decision-making, intuition plays a key role in recognizing subtle patterns that may not be immediately obvious through analytics alone. By refining their ability to tap into this subconscious awareness, surgeons can become more adaptive and effective in the operating room.

○

When we step beyond the labels and categories, we begin to see the beauty of the unseen. The patterns of blood vessels, the beating of the human heart, the workings of the human eye, are all manifestations of a deeper, almost mystical order, the same order that is connected to our thinking mind by intuition. When we truly connect with the human body and the underlying forces that govern it, we cannot but experience a sense of awe and wonder.

# BUDDHA

*Does a surgeon have Buddha nature? . . . Mu.*\*

ME

THE FREEDOM TO CHOOSE—it's wonderful, isn't it? You have it, or at least you *think* you do. You can choose what to wear, where to go, who to meet, what to eat, and more. So many choices, every day, all day long—and most of them are trivial. But what if you had to choose your surgeon? Now there's a choice with real consequences.

---

\* This koan is inspired by Case 1 of *The Gateless Gate*, a 13th-century Zen collection by Wumen Huikai. The monk's question, "Does a dog have Buddha nature?" receives the enigmatic reply, Mu—a response transcending "yes" or "no," pointing beyond conceptual thought to direct realization.

If you're in the medical field, you might ask colleagues for recommendations. If you're not, well, good luck. You'd hope the surgeon is intelligent, skilled, has steady hands, and works with a good team. But you'll never truly know your surgeon because appearances can be deceiving. How they behave in a ten-minute preoperative consultation might be entirely different from how they act behind closed operating room doors. If that time comes, hopefully, you'll be asleep or sedated enough to not know you've made a bad choice.

○

If you meet a buddha in the operating room, hand him the knife. A buddha, from the Sanskrit word *budh* meaning "to awaken," is an individual who is awakened, or has become fully enlightened. Who would you prefer as your surgeon? A surgeon with a temper and a god complex, who yells at staff and believes they are always right? Or a buddha in the OR? The answer is obvious.

The ideal surgeon operates with a calm and meditative mindset, never losing their temper. This creates a positive environment where staff feel comfortable pointing out mistakes. They view unexpected challenges as opportunities for growth and performance. These surgeons are calm and composed, even under pressure. They are often humble and unassuming, focusing on the art of surgery for its own sake. In their presence, the operating room prospers.

A buddha in the operating room would be a surgeon who embodies these qualities. They would be calm, compassionate, and skilled, creating a positive and harmonious environment for patients and staff alike. *Wherever a wise and noble surgeon is found, that operating room prospers.*[†]

○

From the moment they have taken the knife, surgeons have dedicated themselves to their art, seeking perfection in it. It is a life of commitment and discipline. Some find great peace in their work, while others struggle to connect. You sometimes come

---

[†] A play on verse 193 from the *Dhammapada*, a collection of 423 verses attributed to the Buddha, offering concise teachings on ethics, mindfulness, and wisdom.

across surgeons in the community who, despite years of experience, find that surgery doesn't come easy to them. They seem to make the wrong decisions over and over again, don't learn from their mistakes, and when things go bad, find someone else in the room to blame. Surgery should be effortless. Certainly, it takes time to get that way, but it should get that way–unless you get in your own way.

Like roller skating, when you first learned to skate, it was tough. You don't think about them now, but there were a lot of steps you had to learn and master. You had to push off, balance yourself, brake, all while trying not to run over or get run over by somebody else. After a while, though, it got easier. The skates were no longer those separate things on your feet; instead, they were an extension of your body. Skating came effortlessly. You'd glide across the neighborhood like there was nothing between your feet and the ground. The skates were never there. Now, every time you lace them on, you're one with the skates and everything around you—skating zen. The same goes for surgery. There comes a time when the knife that separates you and the patient all merge into one field of consciousness and action.

When a surgeon is truly in control of himself, he experiences his art without consciously forcing it to happen. Being conscious of oneself is required at first so that one understands the art of surgery, but, to truly express oneself as a surgeon, one must move into that state where technique is transcended so that the art emerges from the subconscious, where the surgeon and patient are no longer at two ends of the knife, but instead one reality. When that happens, the surgeon ceases to be conscious of himself. Time is forgotten. The instruments matter but don't really matter. There is only the quietude of the moment which seems to pause in front of you. Completely empty and rid of the self, the surgeon becomes fully one with his technical skills, experience, and years of training. There is no thinking, only responding, and creating. The practice of surgery has become art. Different traditions have different terms for it. Some call it *karma yoga*, some call it *Wu Wei*, the modern psychological term for that state of mind is *flow*, but I like to call it being *zen* in surgery.

○

BUDDHA

One mind, one body.[‡] When the doors close behind you, are you a buddha in the operating room? Do you embrace the moment, or do you run from it? For the buddha, there is no "you," no "patient," only the pathology and the action of surgery. You simply show up, and the surgery is done. In this state, your mind is calm. The moment, the case before you, is fully embraced. The divisions separating mind, hand, and body, you and your environment, disappear. The patient *is* you. There are no unnecessary thoughts, no unnecessary movements of the hand, only complete economy of mind and motion. There is no hesitation, no waiting. There is no ego. The mind is mastered, a tool to achieve an outcome. Nothing else matters. Your awareness expands to encompass all aspects of the surgical procedure, and your hands seem to have a mind of their own, no longer requiring conscious direction. There is no tension—not in your hand, not in the instruments, not in the tissue planes, not in your mind. All move together in harmony, perfectly synchronized. Without doing, the surgery is done. You settle back in your mind, amazed at this action that seems to come from nowhere. You're filled with pure joy. You feel no need for reward or peer

---

[‡] Koan

approval. You have no concern for what others think, and so you are free to do only what is right. You have given of yourself, benefited by whatever came naturally, offering only what was needed for the moment. Your training has disappeared. Your mind is unaware of its surroundings. The "self" has died away. The art of surgery has attained perfection.

Sounds wonderful, doesn't it? But what if that's not you? What if you're something less than a buddha in the OR? How do you get there? Practice, experience, self-awareness—all are necessary, but not enough. Something else is required: the discipline of selfless action. This holds true for anything in life. One must act without attachment to an external goal (like profit or fame), for otherwise, attachment to or identification with any goal other than the task at hand gives rise to a sense of duality between the mind that intends and the hands that execute. The act must be performed for the love of the art alone, without attachment to the fruit of the action, for only then does one find unity in the art. §

---

§ *Karma Yoga*, described in the *Bhagavad Gita* (2.47), emphasizes selfless action: "You have the right to act, but not to the fruits." Rooted in Vedic thought, it advocates detached action as a path to inner harmony and freedom from duality.

○

What is the sound of one hand clapping?** In Zen, *Satori* refers to the experience of seeing one's true nature, a moment of awakening, of comprehension and understanding. For the awakened surgeon, the operating room becomes a sacred space. It's your *sanctum sanctorum*, a place to discover your "self" and truth. But beyond holy places, there are, in fact, only holy moments, moments to experience *Satori*, moments that unfold every time you step into the operating room.

---

** This classic koan invites the mind to contemplate the nature of existence and the illusion of duality. It can serve as a metaphor for the search for enlightenment and the realization of one's true nature.

# EPILOGUE

*The most important thing is to find out
what is the most important thing.*

SHUNRYU SUZUKI

IN LIFE, you have to know where you fit in. You have to be in the right place. That's where you'll find fulfillment. That said, you'll find you're always in the right place—or as the Japanese say, *jijimuge*.* As surgeons, we don't act alone. No one does. We're all

---

* The Japanese Zen Buddhist concept of *jijimuge*, meaning "the unimpeded interpenetration of all phenomena," offers a profound lens through which to view the ephemeral experience of life and being a surgeon. It encapsulates the idea of a universe interconnected without barriers, where all beings and things are inherently unified. This philosophy underscores the harmony between the mundane and the profound.

part of something bigger, and the role we play is the right one for us.

In surgery, there is only one koan: the human body, and the scalpel the key to its mystery. The human body unveiled is, and should always remain, a cause for wonder and reflection. Beneath the flesh, we witness the commonality of all human beings. The practice of surgery reminds us that beneath form and conditioning, we are alike—human beings first, foremost, and forever. We all breathe and bleed the same. The operating table is the great equalizer—there is neither sinner nor saint, only emptiness beneath, the unity of all life. The art of surgery is something that inspires a reverence for life, one that should remain with you as long as you operate and forever after.

Art, like life, never ends. It is ever evolving. Your career, however, is finite. Enjoy the art while you can. To operate, to practice medicine, and to partake in this wonderful thing called life is both privilege and miracle. One day you'll peak, and then you'll begin to slow down. If you're self-aware, your personal process of discovery will continue. You'll learn more about yourself every day until the day you have to hang up your scrubs. None of us will operate forever, but your skills and actions will have consequences that live on through the lives of your patients, the contributions you've made to the art, and those you may have trained. If it's not you, someone, somewhere will be operating, perhaps because of you, carrying on where you no longer could. There is great beauty in the art, for the art is life, and life is undeniably beautiful. To know our days are numbered makes it even more so. To know life in every breath, yours and your patient's, in every heartbeat, and in every pass of your surgical blade — that is *Zen in the Art of Surgery.*

# ACKNOWLEDGEMENTS

No man stands alone. It is due to the kindness of countless others known and unknown to me that I am here today. To all, I am grateful. A special thanks to my dear friend Bill Walz for introducing me to my own conditioning, consciousness, and for the past several decades encouraging me to walk through the *Gateless Gate*—and keep walking.

# CREDITS

Excerpt from *Enter the Dragon* granted courtesy of Warner Bros. Entertainment, Inc.

*The Uncertain Art. Thoughts on a Life in Medicine* by Sherwin B. Nuland. Copyright © 2008. Random House Publishing. Used by Permission of Penguin Random House, LLC.

*Talk to Myself.* Words and Music by Timothy Gatling and Alton Stewart. Copyright © 1989 Wokie Music and Whole Nine Yards Music. All Rights Administered by WB Music Corp. All Rights Reserved. Used By Permission of Alfred Music.

*Zen Mind, Beginner's Mind*, by Shunryu Suzuki. Protected under the terms of the International Copyright Union. Reprinted by arrangement with The Permissions Company, Inc., on behalf of Shambhala Publications Inc., Boulder, Colorado. www.shambhala.com

# ABOUT THE AUTHOR

Saad Shaikh grew up in Irvine, California, and graduated from UCLA with a bachelor's degree in biochemistry. He received his medical degree from the UC Davis School of Medicine and then completed his surgical residency training in ophthalmology at Stanford, followed by a fellowship in retinal surgery at William Beaumont Hospital in Royal Oak, Michigan. He holds several university professorships and has authored several books, book chapters, and academic papers. He has a special interest in mindfulness and the humanistic aspects of medicine, which, ironically, seem to be mostly missing in a modern healthcare system that is often focused on anything but the care and love of humanity. *

In addition to his professional pursuits, Saad is a certified Yoga teacher and enjoys traveling, photography, and documenting his observations about life, medicine, humanity, and whatever else arises in his mind. You can find his articles on his personal webpage.

www.saadshaikh.com

---

* "Wherever the art of Medicine is loved, there is also a love of Humanity."
— Hippocrates

Made in the USA
Monee, IL
02 February 2025

8323474c-21c8-4b6e-b74e-98ad1c7fa3edR01